Me, Teacher, Me........
Please!

Observations about Parents, Students and Teachers and the Teacher-Learning Process

(Second Edition)

Wilbur L. Brower, Ph. D.

Forward by Willie Jolley

Library of Congress Control Number: 00-110606

Me, Teacher, Me........Please! -- *Observations about Parents, Students and Teachers and the Teacher-Learning Process* (**Second Edition**)

Brower, Wilbur L.

1. Adolescent Psychology
2. Education and Training
3. Human Development / Motivation

ISBN: 978-0-9884490-8-4

Correspondence to the author should be directed to:

Dr. Wilbur L. Brower
P. O. Box 565
Trenton, NC 28585

Phone: (252) 448-0132
Cell: (910) 548-0698
E-mail: wlbrower@gmail.com

A REVIEW

In the spate of books about education recently published, Dr. Wilbur L. Brower's ascends to the top above all the rest as refreshingly unique — from its title page to its last page. It is an excellent account of the need to look at how schools, teachers, the bureaucracy, and society relate to children. It is a most creative way of weaving together observations about life in schools.

Dr. Brower is a gifted writer. With clarity and perception, he paints a picture of schools, classrooms and those who inhabit them. This book is not only descriptive writing as its best, but it directs our attention to acceptance of ethnic diversity. As educators, we must discharge our obligations to all students and our society. We may not be able to save them all, but they all are worth saving.

Me, Teacher, Me...Please! is as beautiful as it is wise, as compassionate as it is critical. Dr. Brower lights a candle of hope in an era of educational gloom, where we must commit ourselves to not only closing the achievement gap, but also eliminating the gap. This book is powerful, perceptive and provocative. I highly recommend it for educators, parents and everyone who cares about society's most valuable resource — children.

Thomas L. Stewart
English Facilitator; Teacher of the Year
High School That Works, Coordinator

ALSO BY DR. WILBUR L. BROWER

Possessing the Land (A novel)

Of Life, Love and Learning — Selected Poems and Educational Raps, Rhythms and Rhymes (2012)

English Grammar and Writing Made Easy — Learn to Communicate More Accurately, Clearly and Concisely (2012)

English Grammar and Writing Made Easy (2012)

Personal Care Journal-The Adult Years (2000, co-authored)

A Little Book of Big Principles-Values and Virtues for a More Successful Life (1998 and 2012)

Traffic Signs on the Road of Life (2012), co-authored with Cynthia Brower

Visit the Author's Page:

http://tinyurl.com/ckw5ms8

DEDICATION

To all of you who already give so much of yourselves to help students succeed; and to those who are willing to give even more. For many of your students, you make the difference in their lives.

To all the students who succeed, despite the incredible odds against you; and those students who will achieve incredible heights with patience, nurturing and understanding.

To all of the parents who understand and accept the importance of their role in the development and well-being of their children; and to all the parents who want to help their children to succeed, but don't know how.

It is to all of you that I dedicate this effort.

ACKNOWLEDGEMENTS

I am grateful to numerous people, including parents, school administrators, students and teachers, for what they have allowed me to learn during the time I've spent with them. I am also appreciative of those who have given me encouragement to share with a larger audience some of the things I've learned. Many of you invested time and effort to comment on the tone and tenor of the manuscript and to provide invaluable insights that added to the pleasure and urgency of completing this endeavor. Although some of the things I've written are not flattering, all of you were willing to read my work. Therefore, I am optimistic that we, collectively, can solve the many challenges facing all involved, actively and passively, in the educational enterprise.

A special thanks to all of those who gave me their cogent comments and insights about this effort. I am especially grateful to the school personnel who have seen how STEP-UPP could benefit their students and have taken the risk to implement the *process* in their schools. It is because of the students who have benefitted and who could benefit from the learning that I find the energy and resolve to continue my efforts in the educational sector.

All of the shortcomings are mine alone.

*All the flowers of
all the tomorrows
are in the seeds of today.*

Chinese Proverb

CONTENTS

FOREWORD

Once in a while there is a work that proves to be invaluable for many reasons and has the potential to affect the lives of many people. *Me, Teacher, Me...Please!* is just such a book. This simple but powerful book, no doubt, will transform the lives of students, teachers and parents by the seeds it plants and the fruits it bears.

Dr. Wil Brower has a unique perspective on the issues involving academic achievement, human intellectual development, and students' at-risk behaviors because he works in the trenches, and he understands and thinks in the world of academia. I recommend that you read this book because, in new times, there is a need for new thinking, and even if you don't agree with Dr. Brower's ideas, you can at least appreciate the new level of thinking that he used to achieve this work. With this new thinking, you will grow and, therefore, be able to better help children to do more, be more and achieve more!

Me, Teacher, Me...Please! is one of those rare books that should be required reading for every educator, educational administrator and parent.

—Willie Jolley
President / CEO
Willie Jolley World Wide
Author of *A Setback Is a Setup for a Comeback*

THINGS TO
THINK ABOUT

- Students don't mind working hard; but they do mind being bored with low-quality, rote tasks that engage neither their bodies nor their minds.

- Students must see that tasks lead somewhere — ideally, from what they know or have experienced toward something of importance to them.

- Students learn better in classrooms where teachers have high, but realistic, expectations for them.

- Many students drop out of school very early; they just wait until they're old enough to leave.

- It is difficult to teach a child of whom you are afraid.

- Those who have the power to define tend to assign different groups position of different status and value — e. g., culture, gender, physical characteristics, race, religion, and sexual orientation. These positions often become unquestioned social customs and the "normal" basis of treatment.

- The economic, educational and social status and the value of groups in this country, as well as in many others around the world, was adjudicated and legislated to inferior positions. But, it was made to appear that the groups themselves were inferior.

- People will idealize their own egos by projecting all of the negative and undesirable characteristics on other groups that can be found in any group of human beings. They have difficulty seeing that all the negative and undesirable characteristics are also present in their own reference group. Their own beliefs and ideas about superiority are often substitutes for the reality of their own mediocrity.

- Prejudices distort perception and perspectives, block open and honest communications, increase unrealistic fears and hatred, and interfere with one's ability to understand and work with people who are different.

- Prejudices damage the personalities of the victims and the victimizers, causing confusion and guilt. This affects their development and functioning in a heterogeneous society.

RE-INTRODUCTION

Before this book was published initially in 2002, I had not been a classroom teacher for more than thirty years. Therefore, much of the book's contents were based on my experiences many years earlier as a single parent who had dealings with five different schools in three different states, as a high school teacher nearly thirty years earlier and as an educational and management consultant and trainer for nearly twenty of those years. I have since taught high school English, AVID and Speech and Debate in three different schools that were considered low-performing and low-wealth. It was my personal preference to teach at these schools because of the value I believed I could add. I learned early on that the needs in all of the schools were enormous, much, much greater that I had anticipated, and that essentially all of my portrayal was accurately reflected in the book. Most of my instructional time was spent with students who were experiencing the most difficulty with the structure of the formal written and spoken language. Because of an acute realization of the challenges many of these students faced, I wrote and published, specifically for them, a primer titled *English Grammar and Writing Made Easy*. I was amazed at the number of students and teachers who stated that they found the book critical to their understanding of the language, which validated my decision for working in such schools.

There were many challenges and situations in all of the schools that were frustrating and gave me grave concerns. Some of them are listed below:

- In one school, there were students in the 9th grade *for the third year* but still had only 7 credits, and nobody—counselors, parents, school administrators and students—was saying anything about it.

- One student at another stated that he was an athlete and did not have to do any of my work. Apparently, he had been allowed to operate from that erroneous assumption far too long. He didn't do the work, so he failed!

- A grant evaluator, who wanted me to provide misleading data, stated that my *problem* was that I was concerned about the results when I refused to go along with the idea. The evaluator worked for the company that helped to write the grant and wrote itself in to conduct the assessment / evaluation. After discussing the issue with school administration, I did not detect any sense of concern or outrage.

- Students in one school were allowed to take an Honors English class I taught class when they had never passed any of the state-mandated English and Reading assessments. Nobody at the school could ever explain to me how and why that was allowed to happen.

Since the first edition of the book was published, many more children and their families have fallen into poverty, lost their homes, and have become food-insecure. Violence against children in schools and in greater society has not abated. Politicians at the local, state and national levels have continued to reduce funding for school meals and instructional support. However, the pressure to increase student academic performance outcomes has increased, in many instances to the point that teachers have devised innumerable ways to teach students to *pass* tests, even when they have limited understanding of materials on which they were tested. This, of course, puts teachers in a no-win situation.

This edition essentially is a re-publication of the first edition without the editorial and technical issues that were missed. It is my hope that the reader — parent — student — teacher — school administrator — politician — will find it still just as honest, insightful and troubling. It is also my hope that the reader will find a nugget of truth in it or some consolation in the knowledge that there is much to be done, and that there are many who have the faith that it can and will get done.

Wilbur L. Brower
May 1, 2013

INTRODUCTION

Many of our children today are caught in a deadly undertow, submerged by politics and the politics of education, grinding poverty, low expectations, labeling and tracking, and unbridled and unconscious capitalism, coupled with growing societal indifference to their plight. Some will emerge from these dire and desperate circumstances and go on to lead productive, fulfilling lives; others will never surface to become the healthy and wholesome adults they are capable of becoming, and have a right to become. That many do not reach their full academic, emotional and social potential is a tragedy. Equally tragic is that these children themselves often are blamed for their circumstances and deemed expendable by the very systems that were created to help them. If is because of these children that I have attempted to share here many of my observations and thoughts, with the hope that if one child is helped or better understood, that simple reward is worth the effort I've given this project.

As a product of a "separate but equal" education, I understood early on that the educational process then was designed to curtail or limit my hopes, aspirations and accomplishments of all those like me. I also understood why our teachers and educators demanded the very best from us because they knew the incredible odds against us and the various conveniently-created obstacles we were bound to face. They instilled in us a desire to learn and provided us with the knowledge and skills to be academically competent and confident.

They also instilled in us a value for hard work and a belief in ourselves and our ability to learn. They demonstrated care, concern and love, all of which said we mattered. Their nurturing of us to excel should have removed any doubts that may have been posed by the question of our nature. Despite what appeared to be insurmountable circumstances, there were many clean and convincing examples of what is possible with forces working in concert to achieve desired outcomes.

The following pages were written over a span of several years and reflect what I experienced as a single parent of an African-American male, what I've learned as an educational consultant, and what I've shared as a designer and trainer of learning processes for teachers and students. Additionally, they reflect what I believe is commonsense about human nature and the way people behave or react, based on how they are treated. Many of the concepts, ideas and "learnings" overlap, hopefully forming broad themes that will provoke some thought and discussion. I also felt that compartmentalizing my concerns, observations and thought would detract from the spontaneous and visceral feelings I brought to each and, therefore, would not do the entire work justice. It would be too refined and polished for effective learning.

My comments and concerns have grown out of a personal concern for all children, especially those labeled "at-risk." Although it has been many years since my son was in school—when I baked cookies for bake sales, went on field trips, and tried to do all the those things a "good" parent should do—I still find myself very much involved in the educational lives of many young people around the country, encouraging them to excel academically, to stay in school and out of trouble, and to remain focused. Many of them probably get tired of my mantra… "It doesn't matter where you come from; the most important thing is where you want to go." If we can get these students to believe that and, with our help, work hard toward that goal, they all can succeed. It has to be inculcated within them that they have the capacity and the right to be successful. They need nobody's permission, and they don't have to be afraid to succeed.

Wilbur L. Brower, Ph. D.

1

ME, TEACHER, ME...PLEASE!

Keesha stretches her little hand as high as she can. "Me. Teacher, me," she says. "Please, please! I know the answer."

The teacher looks are Keesha, then looks in the opposite direction at the little girl with the freckles and red hair.

"Oh, Megan, that's a pretty dress you have on today." The teacher asks, "What's the answer?"

Megan's answer is not exactly correct, but the teacher helps her to answer it correctly. "How's that baby brother of yours?" she asks.

Megan beams and says, "He's growing real fast, Teacher. He's this big," while stretching her little arms as far as she can.

Keesha drops her big brown eyes, and then lifts them back up at the teacher with a look of hurt across her round, dark face. "Why won't the teacher call on me?" she asks herself.

The teacher smiles approvingly at some of the students while practically ignoring others. The teacher asks another question and several little hands stretch high. Torn between sitting and standing at the same time, Keehsa waves her little hand to get the teacher's attention. Ignoring Keesha again, the teacher points to the boy whose hand is half up and half down.

"Sean," she said, "You look like you know the answer."

Sean does not know the answer at all. The teacher coaches him to it. "You're such a smart boy, Sean," the teacher says.

He pans his little blue eyes around the room with a demeanor of confidence, then back at the teacher with a look of gratitude.

"Jessica, do you want to give us your answer?" the teacher asks.

The little girls with the long blond hair talks about many different things for more than a minute, then signals her conclusion with, "That's what I think, Teacher."

"That's great, Jessica. Tell your Mom I said, 'Hello,'" the teacher said proudly.

"But, I knew the answer," Keesha says to herself. "The teacher won't call on me. I'm smart, too. I'm as smart as Megan, Sean and Jessica. I have a baby brother *and* a baby sister."

She looks off into the distance while folding her little arms across her chest, as if she's trying to hug herself.

Anticipating the next question, as soon as the teacher begins to ask it, Keesha bolts out of her seat and says, "Teacher, call on me. I know the answer."

The teacher looks at Keesha disapprovingly and yells, "Sit down and be quiet!"

Stunned by the teacher's reactions, the little girl with the big brown eyes and round dark face struggles to hold back her tears.

Again, she couldn't let the teacher know how smart she is. She sits inattentively and passively as the room is abuzz with attempts to get the teacher's attention to answer the next question. She quietly put her head on her desk and begins to twirl one of her long braids.

Startled by the loud call of a name foreign to her, and surprised that all eyes are staring in her direction, the little girl with the big brown eyes and the round dark face looks up in time to see the teacher gaze coldly at her and say, "Kimberly, I said stop daydreaming!"

DIFFERENCES

All people are different. So, we don't automatically fear people who are different. We fear what we have been taught or what we have learned is a negative difference, which makes us skeptical about the differences among people and groups of people.

To ignore people's differences is to never understand who they are, because obvious and not-so-obvious differences do matter in this society. Theses form the very heart and soul of who people are and how they think about, and react and respond to the world around them. When people's differences deviate from a defined norm, they are treated, often unconsciously, as though they don't exist or as if they are virtually invisible.

Differences that are treated in a negative manner cause painful experiences for the subjects of such treatment. The individual will not share these experiences if you have shown or show an inability to understand or don't give them reason to believe you could understand.

Differences that are thought about and treated in a resentful manner often create negative attitudes and behaviors, including emotional, psychological and social deprivation. The predictable result for individuals treated in a scornful manner is cognitive regression.

THE TEACHER AS MANAGER

During a recent trip from Dallas-Ft. Worth, Texas, to Fayetteville, North Carolina, where I live, I had the pleasure of sitting beside one of the town's elementary school principals. She noticed that I was reading *Laying Down the Law – Joe Clark's Strategy for Saving Our Schools*, (Regnery Gateway, 1989), and inquired whether I was an educator. I explained that I was not an educator in the traditional sense, but proceeded to explain to her that much of what I do is really to "educate."

As a former high school and substitute teacher, guest lecturer and visiting professor, and holder of numerous corporate line and staff jobs, I learned so much about the process of education that it serves me well in my current profession as a consultant to management and trainer. Thus, our discussion revolved around the parallel roles of managers and teachers. The richness of our discussion subsequently prompted me to write down these thoughts.

Some would argue that a teacher is not a manager or leader because of the classical definition of the terms. For those, perhaps a more palatable expression and title of these comments might be "the teacher as facilitator." In any event, there are several critical and personal behaviors that a teacher can exhibit to either enhance or inhibit the educational or learning process. Very much like a manager, the teacher ultimately is responsible for the outcomes.

A teacher's personal approachability, presence, persuasiveness and presentation affect the learner. These factors have a direct bearing on the comfort level and rapport established between the teacher and the learner. How a teacher entices or induces a learner to listen and absorb information being presented will determine that learner's motivation to learn. The teacher has to be familiar with the learner's dominant learning style, and must be able to vary information / instructions to meet special needs. (Unfortunately, some teachers are likely to teach the way they learn best.) The clarity and quality of information, and breadth and depth of knowledge about the subject matter should capture the learner's attention and imagination. The student is likely to "tune-out" if there are distortions — too much, too little, or too confusing. (These are factors of which I am mindful as a consultant and trainer.)

Within the social and psychological learning context, a teacher's behavior is a continuous process that affects the learner. In other words, a teacher cannot avoid behaving. The teacher signals numerous messages all the time, even when the teacher thinks she is doing nothing. The slightest non-verbal signal makes an impression on the learner — oftentimes an indelible impression. Learning is likely to be impeded if the learner feels that somehow he is being diminished by the behaviors of the teacher.

Learning is a process of trying. Therefore, learning involves some less-than- successful outcomes — often termed *failures*. An off-hand remark, winch or raised eyebrow at a learner's mistake can signal discouragement. The result can be disengagement and doubt about one's ability to learn. Or, another possible result is that the learner concentrates so heavily on not failing that failure is inevitable, which is known as the classical *Wallenda Effect.*

If the teacher attributes the learner's lack of performance to inherent and unchangeable inabilities, the teacher is not likely to pursue alternatives to help the learner learn. It is the teacher's responsibility to facilitate the learning process and to teach the learner *how* to learn. This involves building self-confidence, supporting risk-taking, fostering curiosity, encouraging independence, enhancing self-worth and expanding capabilities. The success or failure of the learner, to a large extent, represents the teacher's score.

While it may seen unfair that the measurement of a teacher's success should be predicated upon the learner, what other measurement or criterion is there—the teacher's platform skills; knowledge of the subject; knowledge of the psychological and sociological theories? So, not to help the learner to be successful, in effect, is self-destructive for the teacher.

In addition to the technical content of learning, the learner looks to the teacher for, and needs from the teacher, psychic rewards such as encouragement, high expectations and verbal support. Learners want to be assured that they, in fact, can learn, and they look to the teacher to help them with learning strategies. If only five to twenty-five percent of achievement is based upon ability, as research suggests, what else could possibly account for the difference? Similar to the way good manager "shapes" the performance behaviors and environment at work, a good teacher also shapes the performance behavior and constructs an environment conducive to learning and psychologically safe for trying. When this occurs, the behaviors of the teacher and the efforts of the learner will be mutually reinforcing. Then, both the teacher and the learner will get higher scores.

Although I have not taught in a traditional school classroom for many years, I can draw upon my experience there to empathize and, in some cases, to sympathize with today's teacher. While teaching undoubtedly is one of the more emotionally demanding and psychologically draining professions in our society, in my opinion, it is also probably one of the most rewarding, though least respected and under-valued. This is a sad commentary considering that many who love to teach and are masterful at it don't, because they cannot afford to; and some who do teach probably should not be allowed to.

Given the nature and experiences of today's learner, it takes a unique individual who can muster the level of commitment and dedication to facilitate the learning process for many of the learners in our nation's schools. It would appear that those who teach are faced with some unique challenges and great opportunities the average individual would rather forego. Notwithstanding receiving inadequate financial resources and community and institutional support, or being the pawns in political squabbles; or having to be all things to many learners, teachers also are blamed for the state of education. All too often, the focus is on the students who don't achieve, and little or no attention is paid to, or no mention is made of, those who excel—and sometimes excel in spite of very difficult circumstances. And little focus is on the environment, lack of parental involvement and, consequently, the learner's lack of motivation and preparation to learn in a classroom setting.

Though we have known for years the impact of the child's home environment on learning, few innovative strategies are consistently funded to solve this problem. The teacher who does not understand the world of the learner outside the classroom is probably at a serious disadvantage in the classroom. Knowledge of the learner's view of the world and experience base provides the teacher data points and frames of reference to connect with the learner in more meaningful and realistic ways. Without that knowledge, any connection, in all probability, will be superficial and, oftentimes, meaningless to the learner. For example, can the teacher:

- "Taste" the pangs of hunger from the learner who has not eaten for twenty-four hours?

- "Hear" the cry of anger from the learner who refuses to talk?

- "Experience" the trauma and turmoil of the learner who has been emotionally scarred and sexually abused?

- "See" the hopelessness and despair the learner sees everyday and everywhere?

- "Feel" the scourge of inferiority to which the learner is subjected daily?

In other words, understanding where the learner "lives" psychologically and emotionally gives the teacher a head start in facilitating the learning process. Not knowing where the learner "lives" is tantamount to "spitting in the wind" when trying to reach her. It probably will be wasted effort, fraught with discouragement and frustration for the learner and the teacher. In addition to being physically unique, each learner is also unique in terms of experiences, responses, rate and process of discovery, methods of expression, eccentricities, and basic behavior. Therefore, learners should not be forced to fit any particular mold or mode. If each learner's uniqueness is seen as signs of independence and self-confidence, he or she is likely to be appreciated in a different light. Each is a "whole" person, torn between seeking self-identity and conforming to arbitrarily-defined models that often conflict with her or his personal circumstances.

As is the case with the manager's responsibility to manage an employee's behavior to achieve the desired outcomes, it is the teacher's *obligation* to manage, not stifle, a learner's behavior to optimize the learning experience, even when the rewards of the classroom don't mean very much to the learner. Thus, similar to a good manager, a good teacher, among other things:

- Learns some details of the learner's personal circumstances (gets to "know" the learner), and uses that knowledge to enhance, not diminish, the learner's development;

- Provides accurate feedback about the learner's performance outcomes and explores ways to improve and persist after a failure;

- Encourages the learner to strive for excellence;

- Sets high, but realistic expectations and helps the learner to achieve them; and

- Creates an environment of mutual respect and accountability.

It appears that we have to come up with better working definitions of education and teaching, and fashion real-world strategies to ensure that both are achieved. Whatever concepts we may have had about each in the past, they, undoubtedly, are either inappropriate or need modifying for today's learner. If we expect to get better results, the underpinnings of education and teaching must visibly support the rhetoric emanating from most sectors, including business, educational, governmental, labor, parental, etc. Without a broad base of support and constructive involvement, the verbiage makes only for good press and the learner becomes a casualty in an ever-increasing complex society.

4

STUDENTS AND LEARNING

The three main objectives of education are to develop critical thinking, effective communication and intellectual flexibility. Therefore, the educational process should enhance the cognitive and intellectual potential of each student; it should make each student more competitive in the classroom and more productive in life. Nobody is born competent. Human are not born either "dumb" or "smart;" they are born with no knowledge and few capabilities. They are not even born with a language; but most are born with the capacity to speak *languages*.

Similarly, most individuals are born with the capacity to achieve high levels of competence if they are properly encouraged and nurtured, and are expected to do so. All are born with the capacity to develop and to learn. That they do or do not achieve high levels of competence and intellectual development has little to do with their biological or genetic makeup. What appears as intellectual inferiority is more often the result of inadequate or poor education and environmental factors, rather than any fundamental biological or genetic deficiency. Cognitive and intellectual development comes from academic performance and an intellectual self-concept.

It becomes more evident that social acceptance and emotional and interpersonal support are essential ingredients for cognitive and intellectual development. Where there is alienation and a lack of interpersonal support, those who are emotionally unsupported and socially isolated will exhibit defensive-assertiveness behaviors. Assertiveness is often a defensive response to a hostile or inhospitable environment. Experiences of alienation seem to affect the motivation to use basic cognitive skills. In fact, there is likely to be a *deliberate* withdrawal of ambition, competencies and motivation.

Cognitive deterioration or stagnation is a device for self-protection. The diminished effort exhibited is often mistakenly viewed as diminished intellectual capacity. It has been demonstrated repeatedly that the stresses of racial and social isolation are primary factors in thwarting academic and cognitive development. As a consequence, many students will redirect their energies into non-intellectual activities, such as athletics, while others will engage in self-destructive and self-limiting behaviors, such as negative social assertiveness.

When social assertiveness is, or is perceived as, negative, great efforts are made to extinguish it. A reduction in social assertiveness skills reduces interpersonal and personal development. Stifling the assertive tendencies also stifles intellectual abilities; and it can also induce social passivity. The challenge for the educator is to be ever mindful of those influences on the cognitive and intellectual development of each student and groups of students.

Each student should experience feelings of belonging and of having academic successes. The learning environment should be structured for the encouragement and support for academic and intellectual gains. It also should help to develop intellectual self-confidence, good study habits and positive social assertiveness. Additionally, it should be structured for academic involvement and a commitment to education and personal improvement. A supportive environment enhances the competitive and intellectual potential of each student. If such an environment does not exist, many students will slip into social withdrawal and will avoid knowing and discovering what they are capable of doing.

5

BELIEVING IS SEEING:
THE POWER OF EXPECTATIONS

*"The difference between a lady and a flower girl
is not how she behaves but how she's treated."*

In George Bernard Shaw's play *Pygmalion* (The
Hollywood movie based on the play was *My Fair
Lady*), Eliza Doolittle explains a very sophisticated
concept in a very simplistic way. In essence, the
character Eliza was saying that if a flower girl is
treated like a flower girl she will always be one; but
if she is treated like a lady she will *become* one.

Popularly known as "The Pygmalion Effect"
or "Self-Fulfilling Prophesy," one of the earliest
accounts of the concept is found in Greek Mythology.
The sculptor Pygmalion hated women, yet he
carved a statue of a woman who was so beautiful
that he fell in love with it. Pygmalion became so
obsessed with the statue Galatea that he treated it
like a real woman; and he believed that the statute
would come to life. He also prayed to Aphrodite,
the Greek Goddess of Love and Beauty, to bring
the statue to life to become his wife. Aphrodite
was very sympathetic to Pygmalion's plight and,
therefore, granted him his desire. Pygmalion's
belief and false prophesy that the statue would
come to life and, thus behaving as if it were true,
caused the fulfillment of the prophesy

The generally accepted definition of a self-fulfilling prophesy is a situation in which originally false information causes a new behavior, resulting in the false information becoming true. The Self-Fulfilling Prophesy concept has been experimented with in settings such as classrooms (See *Pygmalion in the Classroom: Teacher Expectation and Pupil Intellectual Development*, Holt Publishing, 1968); and it has been written about in educational, management, medical, psychological and sociological literature.

In a 1948 *Antioch Review* (Vol.8, pp. 193-210) article titled "Self-Fulfilling Prophesy," sociologist Robert Merton provided one of the earliest frameworks for understanding the phenomenon and established a classical operational definition. A survey of various disciplines points up one commonality: people in subordinate positions tend to live up to or down to the expectations of the individual (s) in authority or superior position. As Sterling Livingston points out (See *Harvard Business Review*, July-August, 1969, Vol. 47, No. 4, 81-9; and *Harvard Business Review*, September-October, 1988, Vol. 66, No. 5, 121-130), there seems to be a law that causes the subordinate to meet those expectations. There is also the belief that people are motivated to behave or perform because they have an *expectation* that they will be better off by having done what was expected of them.

In any event, the poser of others' expectations about the behavior and performance is profound, and the manner in which people in authority or superior positions treat subordinates is influenced subtly and unconsciously by what they *expect* of them. It is as though subordinates behave and perform as they believe they should, based on the expectations they received, not necessarily as they are told they should. Some of the cues employed to set expectations include: eye contact or lack of it; the frequency and quality of interpersonal interactions; smiles, head nods, touches, encouragement or lack thereof; the nature and quality of feedback; tone of voice, voice inflections; physical distance maintained; and general body language.

Studies have shown that communication occurs on three levels, consisting of *verbal* (the content of the message), *vocal* (how the message is articulated), and *visual* (what the sender looks like while articulating the message). Studies also show that the sender sends and the receiver receives seven percent of the message verbally, thirty-eight percent vocally and fifty-five percent visually. So, the behavior of one in authority has more impact than what one says, and the subtle and unconscious messages can have positive and negative outcomes. Many expectations emanate from biases and prejudices, recognized and unrecognized by the individual and show up unexpectedly.

Throughout greater society, expectations, often called triggers, are set for individuals based on who they are; what they look like; where they come from; their style and language; their degree of sophistication in social situations; their socio-economic status, etc. These triggers can cause individuals to be disparaged, pigeonholed, prejudged and treated differentially. The belief and expectation is that these individuals are undisciplined, unintelligent, unmotivated and unsophisticated; all of their behaviors and characteristics are seen as negatives. In many respects, the classroom is a microcosm of greater society and its way of thinking. Within this environment, students often are categorized, viewed and, consequently, treated based on the same triggers.

As a result, teachers and school administrators can become victims of their own thinking about these students and their ability to learn. Their beliefs about these students and their mental abilities can close their minds to the potential that these students have to learn anything they want to learn and are *motivated* to learn. Believing that sagging pants, body paint and piercing, cornrows and crew cuts, colorful language and swaggers determine students' ability to learn will undoubtedly cause them to see an *inability* in these students and, therefore, expect less of them. Students recognize this immediately and will often exaggerate behaviors and styles, particularly if they believe their behaviors and styles are sources of exasperation and irritation for those making judgments about them.

These are expressions and statements that have nothing to do with the students' ability to achieve high academic performance if they are challenged to do so. In fact, many of these students are academically gifted and very talented. They've learned to behave and dress in ways to fit in with their peers for social acceptance. Some have also learned that by behaving and dressing in certain ways, they will not be expected to do their best.

It has been shown, time and time again, that students learn best in classrooms where teacher expectations are high. It doesn't matter where the students come from, what they look like, their socio-economic status, etc.; they can be moved to higher academic and intellectual ground. At any given point in their schooling, however, they may not be at the same academic level as someone who has been advantaged economically and socially; but it does not mean the disadvantage cannot be overcome with the development of their potential and greater cultural and social exposure for them. If teachers believe only the negatives about these students, that is all they will see and expect. Rarely will they get more than they, the teachers, expect!

6

EMOTIONAL AND SOCIAL LEARNING:

A PRIORITY FOR "AT-RISK" BOYS

The general plight of the nation's children is a growing concern. The concern tends to center around issues of health conditions, nutrition and parental care. The condition of children appears to be more worrisome, now that their plight is chronicled in the popular press and highlighted via the electronic media. This includes cuts in Federal and State social "safety nets" for the poor; violence among children, even in small-town America; and lack of basic medical care for poor children. More bothersome still is the issue of the lack of educational achievement generally, especially during time when the demand for technical competence and increased skills and capabilities is growing.

Based upon several governmental and privately-funded studies, the workforce is becoming more diverse, and work in the future will require higher-skilled workers. Workers will have to learn *how* to learn, be adaptable and flexible; know how to work cooperatively and how to influence and negotiate; and to exhibit self-confidence, self-worth and high self-esteem. While these implications are far-reaching for all, they are particularly troublesome for Blacks generally, and Black males especially, when they are considered in context with the current trends, and measured against some rational benchmark. The focus of these comments, therefore, will be on Black boys, and are not intended to minimize the challenges of all boys and girls, irrespective of ethnic background.

Consider some of the following statistics gleaned from sources such as the U. S. Census Bureau, the Carnegie Foundation, President's National Commission for Excellence in Education, and the Center for Disease Control and Prevention:

- Black newborn males are twice as likely to die before age one than white newborn males.

- Between birth and age five, twice as many Black children die as White children.

- Black boys make up fifty-five percent of boys under five with AIDS.

- Black males five to thirty-four years of age are nearly five times more likely to die from asthma than are Whites, and one and a half times more likely than Black females.

- Approximately forty-five percent of all Black children live in families with incomes below the poverty level.

- Nearly sixty percent of all Black children born in 1989 were born to unwed mothers.

- More than half of all Black children are reared in fatherless homes.

- Approximately forty-three percent of all Black males under age six live at or below the federal poverty level.

BLACK BOYS AND TEENAGERS

- Black boys between the ages of fifteen to nineteen are eleven times more likely than White males to die by gunfire.

- Approximately forty-four percent of Black seventeen year olds are functionally illiterate.

- The Black high school dropout rate is about forty percent in many urban areas, and approaches fifty percent in some inner cities.

- More than fifty-five percent of all Black males fail to complete high school.

BLACK MEN

- More than forty percent of the inmates in federal and state prisons are Black.

- There are more Black men in prison and correctional facilities than there are in college.

- Almost one in four Black men is either in prison, in jail, on probation, or on parole.

- There are approximately twenty-eight Black males per one hundred thousand incarcerated for some period of time, compared to two White males and less than one Black or White female.

- The number of Blacks who lost their lives due to 'Black-on-Black" violence in 1989 was equal to the number of Black servicemen killed during the entire Vietnam Conflict.

While it is assumed that the family is the first line of defense relative to the nurturing and caring of its offspring, this very often is not the case. In fact, several of the Possible Precipitators in **Figure 1**, *At-Risk / Intervention Model*, speak to the defenselessness of the family and the abdication of family and parental responsibility. This is often compounded by the lack of financial resources and structural support; societal attitudes, beliefs and expectations; and perceptions created by results and symptoms, rather than the root causes.

AT-RISK / INTERVENTION MODEL

POSSIBLE PERCIPITATORS	Low family and teacher expectations — Differential treatment — Lack of parental control / involvement — Dysfunctional family situation — No advocate or sponsor — Negative peer pressure — Impoverished backgrounds — Lack of positive role models — Strong materialistic values — Violent experiences — Poor academic households — Negative self-image — Lack of encouragement — Emotional / physical / sexual abuse
RESULTS	Short-term orientation — Anger — Defiance — Aggressive behavior — Apparent laziness toward academic learning — Unwillingness to try — Lack of cooperation — Resentment — Misbehavior — "Don't Care" attitude — Self-defeating behaviors — Struggle for power and recognition — Little sense of own ability to change — Denial of responsibility for own behavior

INTERVENTION OBJECTIVES	Build on strengths – Change self-image – Change behavior – Encourage cooperation – Foster academic success – Instill confidence – Teach concern for self and others – Teach accepting responsibility for own actions and behaviors – Explore career and personal options – Enhance learning experience – Develop "caring" attitudes

Figure 1

Numerous boys are labeled "at-risk" at birth or early during their school experience. While many tend to make academic and social progress at the equivalent rate as their cohorts during grades K-3, substantial changes begin to occur around grade 4. Known as the "fourth grade syndrome," a combination of changes in their behavior and treatment of those behaviors is a perplexing problem that, for the most part, goes unattended. Without an understanding of how to negotiate and without acquiring the skills to trade in this society, including in school, too many "at-risk" boys become grim statistics and societal casualties before they legally become men. They drop out of school and the learning process very early. In other words, they dropout early, but just wait until they are old enough to leave.

Anecdotal information and probably quantitative data from any school with a significant number of Black boys also would suggest that Black boys are likely to be given harsher punishment for outright violating or pushing the parameters of school rules. They are more likely to be labeled or stigmatized with such adjectives as "BEH," "LD,"

"Dumb," or other limiting names. Often they are consciously or unconsciously left out of the academic interchange, but encouraged, if not coerced, to become an intricate part of the *athletic* dimension of the school experience. Therefore, expectations for them become very clear. Consequently, the "Results" identified in Figure 1 should not be surprising.

Within the context of the learning, growth and development, the focus tends to be on how well one does on mental aptitude tests; and society tends to place greater value on those who score higher on such tests, which purport to measure one's "cognitive ability" or one's "intelligence." But, do they? By wading into the murky area of testing and intelligence, we are forced to ask many questions tangentially related:

1. Can "intelligence" be measured?

2. Is intelligence related to cognitive skills — primarily quantitative and verbal?

3. Do intelligence tests really measure intelligence; or do they measure what one has learned?

4. Do they measure one's ability to learn?

5. Do "intelligence" tests measure privilege or potential?

To be sure, these questions evoke additional questions, and the subordinate question: What is the primary purpose of a cognitive skills test? This question notwithstanding, however, will the community, and in deed the society, survive if there is no focus on or effort devoted to a student's emotional / psychological and social growth and development?

Humans are social beings who conduct themselves on the basis of friendships and interpersonal interactions. Friendships and interpersonal interactions are enhanced or thwarted by various socio-psychological factors that 1) give us self-definition of others; and 2) determine how we relate to ourselves and how we relate to and interact with others. Also, cognitively and psychologically, we are continually" shaped" or "warped," as the case may be, by our social setting. Viewed in this context, it seems that students' emotional / psychological and social growth and development take on added importance, and that these dimensions of development, by necessity, must form a balanced coalition with cognitive / intellectual development to facilitate the student's overall progress.

Given the complexity of our society, the increasing push toward technical competence, the uncertainty about the future, and the constant change in social values, can it be assumed that an individual will become effective and masterful if the focus of development is limited almost exclusively to the cognitive / intellectual? The long-term prospects for the individual and society probably are not very good. While a well-balanced life probably includes physical and spiritual growth and development, these dimensions will not be addressed here.

It is my opinion that cognitive / intellectual, emotional / psychological and social growth and development are three *interdependent* dimensions that form a dynamic and symbiotic relationship necessary to energize, sustain and propel healthy, wholesome individuals in the pursuit of happiness and personal achievements. **Figure 2**, *Dimensions of Development*, is a representation of these relationships. Although the three referenced dimensions of development cannot be compartmentalized or divorced from each other and studied in isolation, an overview of each as a separate entity can provide some insight into and an understanding of how each affects the other.

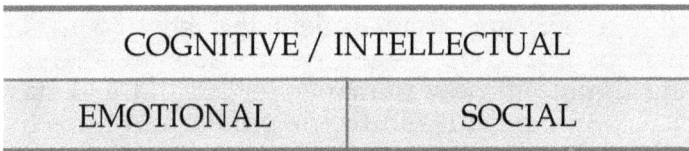

COGNITIVE / INTELLECTUAL	
EMOTIONAL	SOCIAL

Figure 2: Dimension of Development

Extensive documentation and research exist on cognitive and intellectual development, especially in children. While the area of study advances many theories and lays the foundation for understanding thought and how information is processed, there are several key precepts. Specifically:

- Cognitive growth is influenced by internal and external factors.

- The integration of information into problem solving results in the use of larger and more complex units of information to solve more complex problems.

- The cognitive development process is facilitated more by intellectually stimulating environments than by intellectually sterile environments.

- Values orientation and language are cultural factors that influence cognitive growth.

The cognitive process denotes logic, the conservation of qualities, weights, heights and numbers; perception, judgment, and creative thinking; meaning, memory, psycho-linguistics, deductive and inductive reasoning, and abstract thinking. In an increasingly complex society, those who have developed sufficient cognitive / intellectual skills are better able to make sense of it all. They see how all the pieces of the jigsaw puzzle fit together, and they understand how to make them work. They generally are able to analyze and figure out how to maneuver around and stay clear of mine fields, obstacles, pitfalls and traps by being intellectually mobile. Cognitive / intellectual development provides one the necessary tools to anticipate the future and to prepare for it. It is a valued and respected asset in this society.

One of the postulates of sociology is that we all have socio-genic needs—that is the desire to belong to groups, and to be accepted and loved by the group. The groups whose opinion we value and whose judgment and praise we seek typically become the groups with whom we identify, or our reference groups. We look for recognition and response from the groups, and we receive many of our social values and self-concept from them. Groups form along religious beliefs, familial relationships, racial identity, ideology, etc., and they have a powerful impact on who we are. Therefore, the "self" is not inherited, but is *acquired*, to a large extent, by groups and their culture.

What then is culture? Culture is defined as the learned and shared behavior of a group, or a common way of life. Culture is learned through a group process and passed on from generation to generation. Many of our attitudes, behavioral characteristics, beliefs, feelings, habits, and opinions are shaped by our reference group and culture. Our reference groups pass on to us strong cues about who we are and what we can hope to be. They mold our thinking and our personality.

Ethnocentrism, which is the preferential feelings members of a reference group have for their own culture, characterizes the American society, especially along gender and racial lines. It tends to be more cultural in other societies. Such feelings have given rise to social distancing between and among groups, and they have served as divisive forces. The ultimate and predictable result is conflict, particularly if one group has had unfair and unwarranted advantage and begins to lose it; or the group recognizes that their cultural beliefs may not be sacrosanct.

Social development entails an understanding of others' cultural and social heritage and effectively integrating them with our own to dissipate social distancing and to form unifying forces across reference groups. Social development accomplishes many objectives. For example:

- Creates camaraderie and esprit de corps
- Builds group bonding and solidarity
- Engenders trust and cooperation
- Promotes sharing ideas and information
- Facilitates open and honest communication
- Stimulates giving and receiving a sense of belonging
- Encourages adaptability and flexibility

Social development is important for students who are expected to function effectively in a global society. It is also important for adults who are charged with helping students toward that end. When adults are socially distanced from their students, it is often difficult for them to relate to, understand, and give the students the skills and tools they need to cope within their own reference group and within the greater society.

Our emotional / psychological makeup is the cornerstone of who we are. The emotional / psychological side of humans has been subjected to scrutiny and debate for many years. It is rather conclusive that unless a person is without feelings or emotions, he or she will respond to stimuli. The human emotional / psychological development process is influenced by a multitude of factors, including the social setting, cognitive stimulation, spiritual teachings and physical effort. We all have a range of emotional responses to, or a reservoir of feelings toward stimuli, and the responses or feelings are unique to each individual. The emotional / psychological development process is dynamic and is continually evolving. Unlike our physical features, which are basically "fixed," our emotional / psychological dimension is subject to modification and fine-tuning.

We often equate emotional / psychological growth and development with "managing" our primitive emotions and responses, or achieving a balance between the peaks and valleys in our feelings or emotional repertoire. This entails repressing some feelings that are "naturally" high and building up or accentuating other feelings that are "naturally" low. Feelings and emotions we must manage include anger, anxiety, attitude; autonomy, avoidance, bashfulness, crying; empathy, envy, fear; frustration, guilt, grief; helplessness, horror, intimacy; jealousy, joy, love; pain, pleasure, prejudice and antipathies; rigidity, shame and sympathy.

The ultimate goal of emotional / psychological growth and development is "emotional maturity," which is infinite. Emotional maturity is a never-ending process through which we grow in our ability to accept, appreciate, respect, tolerate and understand ourselves and others. It is a process through which we grow in our capacity to direct ourselves, rely on ourselves, and take responsibility around issues affecting our lives. Therefore, emotional / psychological growth and development promotes:

- An understanding of self
- Being comfortable with self
- Self-acceptance
- Proper definition of self in context with others and the world-at-large
- A sense of well-being
- Self-esteem and self-confidence
- A clear self-image and self-concept
- Adaptability

Having emotions is very much a part of living. How we chose to deal with our emotional and psychological health will determine how and to what degree we grow. All too often, individuals who are affected by many of the Precipitators referenced in **Figure 1** will behave in ways that appear to be illogical and irrational to the casual observer. Without understanding the impact of the emotional / psychological dimension of their development, "they" will become the problem, rather than their *behaviors*. Erroneous judgment will be made about their ability to learn.

It has been my experience that an intervention designed to address the emotional and social dimensions of learning can enhance one's personal mastery skills, giving the individual a greater sense of control, a higher level of self-confidence, and positive self-expectations. The individual also acquires a more realistic way to think about cognitive capabilities. I believe that emotional and social development is the foundation for cognitive development, and that to concentrate only on cognitive development can be a formula for educational disaster. The STEP-UPP, discussed in Chapter 10, has several Intervention Objectives, indicated in Figure 1. It is open to all "at-risk" young adults and can be implemented with a minimum of disruption or interruption to the normal school schedule. The payoff can be enormous for participating students, the school and society. The results are more emotionally and socially "healthy" and academically secure students, and reduced emotional and monetary drain on the society.

THE FALLACY OF STUDENT FAILURE

As an educational and business consultant and as a school volunteer during the past fifteen years, I've been privileged to work closely with a number of students who have been labeled "at-risk" or "failures." During my involvement with theses students, I have become keenly aware that they are neither "at-risk" nor "failures" because of who they are or what they *currently* cannot do. On the contrary, these students are put at-risk or they are failed because of what is not done with and for them in the educational system and through the teaching-learning process.

I believe, therefore, that the idea of student failure, in and of itself, is a fallacy. More specifically, I have perceived that this fallacy has evolved from three primary sources:

1. Parents and guardians who abdicate their responsibilities and leave the appropriate socialization and complete education of their children to the educational system;

2. Educators who set highfalutin, theoretical, and impractical goals that emphasize

testing and labeling students rather than educating them academically and socially; and

3. Politicians who have abused the educational system as means to achieve political objectives.

First and foremost, parents and guardians put their children at-risk by assuming that the educational system is working in their best interest. When they fail to attend parent-teacher meetings and fail to be involved with the child's schooling experience, this has the appearance of, and often is interpreted as, the parents or guardians having no interest in their child's academic achievement, general well-being and future success. This apparent lack of interest is reinforced if the child enters the educational system without the basic learning and social skills expected of him or her.

If the child does not possess a reasonable degree of self-control and willingness to learn, she undoubtedly will be labeled and tracked as an under-achiever on the front end of the educational experience. If the parent or guardian disciplines the child differently than the school or fails to correct inappropriate behaviors, the child will often experience behavioral problems that cause him to be labeled "at-risk." Educators, in this case, are reluctant to impose discipline for fear of physical or verbal retaliation from the child, the parent and others in the school community. Furthermore, recent laws championing students' rights fail on the discipline front. Teachers who care enough to hold the line may find themselves the target of physical or verbal abuse charges.

Secondly, educators put students at-risk and ensure their failure by focusing on periodic tests and measurements rather than on progressive and continual learning. The unrelenting pressure for students to pass tests, at the expense of acquiring foundational knowledge and skills, will almost guarantee their failure in the future. The tests and measurements will overshadow true understanding and learning *how* to learn. Therefore, the trademark of the teaching-learning process should not be based on theoretical and impractical goals and objectives. Instead, the trademark of the educational system should be an open-door policy that accepts the student "as-is" and teaches her to learn and to think.

Highfalutin goals, objectives and mission statements have no practical value if little is actually done to ensure that all students participate in and benefit from the educational process in a constructive and wholesome manner. Goals, objectives and mission statements do not educate students! Educators and greater society must do it by helping students achieve their full potential, instead of labeling them "at-risk" or "failures." Students labeled "at-risk" are those who are likely to leave school at any age without the academic, emotional, social and / or technical / vocational skills to lead productive lives.

I contend that these students are put "at-risk" and are allowed to become "failures" by the educational system. To eradicate this fallacy of student failure, educators must instill in these students self-confidence, self-motivation and self-worth. In addition, educators must focus on foundational knowledge and continual learning as means or ways to become more capable, rather than on "testing" just to gauge what they don't know and subsequently "labeling" students to decide what they might not be capable of learning. The re-mediation process used to help students who have less than successful academic outcomes is often a regurgitation of students' past learning experiences. Much needs to be done to create new experiences for these students that will: 1) allow them to learn according to their style of learning; 2) include experiential learning approaches implemented by teachers trained in this mode of learning; and 3) practical experiences that enrich the learning task as a whole.

Third, the fallacy of student failure has evolved from politicians who have abused the educational system as a means to achieve political objectives. Ironically, many of the politicians and individuals who control school boards are not educators and probably will spend time in a classroom only for a photo opportunity. The issue of who should be educated has been a perennial one, and the fervor surrounding it continues to escalate. The history of the United States, I believe, substantiates the fact that politicians have been vigilant in their appeasement of those who had the most economic and political clout and social standing regarding the education of their children, and less vigilant or totally inattentive to those who had none. The history of education, coupled with the history of voting, provides an interesting perspective on the *politics* of education.

I perceive that it is incumbent upon politicians to end their role in student failure. They must face the reality that all students do not enter the educational system and the teacher-learning process at the same level. However, this should not deny some students the opportunity to acquire foundational knowledge and to develop basic skills that facilitate their continual learning, and the necessary funding and interventions for the knowledge and skills to be acquired.

Research reveals that student under-achievement, which is not addressed properly, puts them at-risk and ensures their failure. For example, research with third-grade students shows that, if....

- a poor child attends school composed largely with other poor children;
- is reading a year behind the third grade;
- has been retained, or "left behind;"
- is from a low socio-economic background;

His or her chances of graduating from high school are near zero!

It is around the third-grade when students begin to see themselves as either learners or non-learners. Research also shows that eighty percent of all prison inmates are high school dropouts, and many of them have grown up in impoverished environments.

When students are achieving below grade-level, funds must be made available to teach them how to achieve at or above grade-level; they should not be merely told to achieve, but *how* to achieve. Many of the behaviors exhibited by students labeled "at-risk" emanate from their frustrations. They become frustrated due to subtle and overt messages that remind them that they cannot be smart because of their deficiencies. Students' negative behaviors often become defense mechanisms to protect their self-esteem and self-worth. Their deficiencies are not statements of what they are capable of becoming, but statements about their *current* level of academic and intellectual development.

Rather than address what is *causing* the behaviors, it is often easier to label the student *as* the behaviors. If students are defined by their behaviors, then there is justification for making no significant changes. Therefore, few or no resources are allocated for this purpose. There is something wrong with a society when politicians are allowed to declare that no resources are available to prevent or intervene in a learner's at-risk behaviors, when some of the preventions and interventions cost only pennies or a few dollars. Sylvan Learning and other successful programs are inaccessible to many of these students because of cost.

Conversely, the same politicians can easily find thousands of dollars to incarcerate that same "at-risk" learner for many years for minor social transgressions for which effective preventions and interventions could have corrected. In fact, some states today are looking at student behaviors in the second and third grades and projecting how many prisons will be needed to house or warehouse these children by the time they become young adults!

Investors today are encouraged to invest in companies that construct and operate prisons, with the expectation and promise they will receive hefty returns on their investment. Ironically, these companies make up the "corrections industry." So, I have to ponder the question: Is there any public or private, non-monetary incentive to prevent and intervene in behaviors that are easily correctable? I believe the "corrections industry" does little, if anything, to correct the behaviors, but they get billions of taxpayers' dollars annually for this purpose. There is no mistaking that there are many people imprisoned who deserve to be and should never be allowed freedom again. This includes young adults. But, there are far too many students who find themselves on the wrong track—the one headed to prison—and little is done to get them off. In fact, some of the inattention or negative attention they receive facilitates their ride to prison. Continually building prisons to accommodate them is not a viable solution to dealing with the problem.

While we, as a society, might not be able to purchase every student into a high socio-economic status, politicians should advocate that, as an enlightened society, we have not become adept at developing students' potential, and mandate that more resources are allocated for that purpose. We can teach every child to read, if he or she is able to speak the language. We can also teach every child basic mathematical skills. We can help each student to earn a comfortable economic and social lifestyle by helping her to acquire basic skills. If we fail to educate all students, the whole society will continue to suffer the consequences of destructive and negative behaviors and results.

It is easy to lose sight of the fact that young adults are still children, trying to discover who they are and what they think they want to do. If those in helping positions and professions, i. e. administrators, counselors, politicians, teachers and parents, would take the time to look behind the oftentimes disrespectful, hard and harsh exterior of these so-called "at-risk" students, they could hear the voices of the scared children crying out for help. Many of these children's attitudes and behaviors are grossly exaggerated because this is what gets attention, albeit, most of it negative. Their attitudes and behaviors are likely to be exaggerated to impress their peers, to challenge authority and to vie for power. This acting out of bravado often disguises itself as dangerous, menacing and threatening. It is often assumed that the attitudes and behaviors, which are socially-sanctioned, must receive the severest form of punishment. While such punishment often includes denial of opportunity to participate in extra-curricular activities and going on school trips, these students are the ones who would probably benefit the most from those types of cultural exposures and social interactions.

And, often the punishment is meted out based on the most negative, stereotypical beliefs about the student, rather than on the true nature of or cause of the attitudes and behaviors. Hence, one cannot look at the attitudes and behaviors of students and make accurate assessments about what is going on inside them. Students can display attitudes and behaviors that are socially-sanctioned, and are apparently considered normal, but commit unspeakable acts of violence against themselves and/or against others. This was made abundantly clear with the incidents of school violence in Jonesboro, Arkansas; Littleton, Colorado; Conyers, Georgia; West Paducah, Kentucky; Pearl, Mississippi; Springfield, Oregon; and Moses Lake, Washington.

It is imperative, therefore, that parents and guardians realize that if they do not impose or provide some structure in the child's home environment, the criminal justice system will do so later, and they will have little, if anything, to say about it. They will have to abdicate most of their rights as parents and guardians, while fueling a juvenile justice system that is not designed to work in the best interest on their children.

Parents also must teach their children achievement behaviors. If not, the educational system will probably treat them with indifference.

If they do not come to school ready to learn and to behave, they are quickly put on an alternative educational track that runs parallel with and into the "corrections system." Instead of making students pawns in their dealings, politicians must support educators in an effort to help all students realize their real potential and instill in them feelings of self-worth, feelings of belonging and a sense of being connected, in addition to teaching them knowledge and skills. Denying students the cognitive, emotional and social components of their development will not only put them at-risk or guarantee their failure, it will put us all at-risk and guarantee the failure of society as a whole.

I conclude, therefore, that student failure, to a great extent, is a combination of parental irresponsibility and the fallacious, though unintended, brainchild of educators and politicians. Students who are put at-risk and / or failed by parents, educators and politicians become a threat to society, and may ultimately cause society to be at-risk and / or become a failure. Talking about student failure and playing the blame game is time wasted if no subsequent action is taken to ensure their success. This wasted time should be spent teaching students *how* to learn and showing them how to develop emotionally and socially. Students who are not taught how to grow and develop emotionally and socially often have difficulty developing academically. If all the emphasis is on their academic development, to the exclusion of their emotional and social development, it is almost certain that their academic development will be truncated; thus, they are put at-risk and failed by parents / guardians, educators and politicians.

We must do better as a civilized society!

CREATING THE MINORITY
ACHIEVEMENT GAP

Several months ago, I observed a very disturbing scene in a classroom designed for "transitional" students. Of approximately ten male students in it, two were boxing, four were playing cards, and one was walking around the room poking the ceiling with a broom handle. After questioning the students about what they were doing, the student who was poking the ceiling stated matter-of-factly, "They don't expect anything from us anyway." Incidentally, this same student, a seventh grader at the time, had some severe skills deficiencies that should have been corrected when he was in the second grade.

These basic deficiencies notwithstanding, he was insightful enough to know that very little, if anything, was expected of them. The vast majority of these students were either African-American or Native American and, according to the school administration, they were learning "life skills." It was clear to me that no learning was taking place that had any academic, economic or social value. So, I couldn't understand what was meant by "life skills." After talking with their teacher, other teachers at the school and the guidance counselor, I learned that the behaviors those students were displaying were a hundred percent improvement over a few weeks earlier because, under the current teacher who had been with them only a few weeks, there were no long any referrals for disciplinary problems.

That scene and images of these young people forced some nagging questions to sift through my mind and prompted me to speculate and wonder about what is going on in classrooms populated with students who are not considered academically gifted or are labeled "EC," "LD," "Slow Learner," "Not College Material," and other labels that signal what is expected of them and how they are to be treated. The scary thought that surfaced time and time again was that the achievement gap so often talked about was not a natural phenomenon, but a situation created by what is done and not done for and with different students, based on who they are and what is expected of them. Just maybe the young man had it exactly right: If you expect nothing from students, that's what they will give you.

Some of the questions that nagged me included:

1. What percentage of the students in "transactional" or low-track classes are minority and / or from lower socio-economic backgrounds?

2. What objective criteria are used to decide placement in such classes?

3. Do the criteria determine what students have learned or what they are capable of learning?

4. Are students targeted for these classes primarily because of their culture, family background and language?

5. Once students are labeled or targeted for less challenging academic tracks, what is the likelihood that they will ever overcome those labels?

6. What happens within schools and the entire educational system that might contribute to unequal educational opportunities and outcomes, causing the achievement gap?

7. Are there beliefs that these students are *genetically* inferior to other students?

8. What are the educational expectations for these students?

9. How does this influence *what* and *how* they are taught?

10. How does this influence the cognitive and intellectual processes they are expected to use?

11. What role does this play in their access to knowledge and positive learning experiences within the school?

12. Are some students getting higher-quality course content, better instructional techniques and more learning time than others?

13. Do teachers perform better for and with some students than they do for and with others?

14. How do all these factors affect learning outcomes?

There were many additional questions that flowed from there, pointing to a constellation of factors and forces that require exploration and systematic study, with an attempt to determine why the academic achievement of minority students, as a group, lags that of Asian and White students. The qualifier "as a group" is important to note because many minority students outperform non-minority students. While there may be no easy method to collect empirical evidence to test my hypotheses, my intuitive sense tells me that there is some validity to my assumptions and observations; and that there is some causal relationship between the differential treatment of students and the academic achievement gap. However, the recurrent questions were sufficient enough to keep me busy for some time just thinking about and proposing some plausible and possible answers to and explanations for them.

From casual observations I've made in several schools, it appears that vocational and non-academic classes are disproportionately populated by minority and / or socio-economically disadvantaged white students. While such designations may not be used officially in many schools, I suspect that they, in fact, are in use *unofficially* to make distinctions between and among students. In fact, these distinctions often are made implicitly right in the classroom, with the academically-gifted sitting in front of the room, and the others, most of whom are minority, sitting in the rear. Not only does the color difference and physical separation stand out, but, in many instances, there are stark differences in how the teacher interacts with the two groups. Students sitting in the front are engaged in serious learning with instructional dialog and positive interactions, while those sitting in the rear are not acknowledged, are allowed to be inattentive, to disengage or even to sleep. In other words, these students can do almost anything, as long as they're not too disruptive. They may as well not be there because they are excluded from the learning process by default. Of course, when the distinctions are official, there are separate classrooms for the students, and there are huge differences between how they are treated and what they are taught.

While the practice of separating students, based on assumptions and beliefs about their ability to learn certain types of materials, is long-standing, one has to wonder about the pedagogical soundness of it. The practice of segregating students, consciously or unconsciously, creates an academic, economic and social stratification, setting in motion a cause-and-effect relationship that is self-perpetuating and self-reinforcing. Those who end up at top tend to receive the very best the educational system has to offer, while those at the bottom get what is left, in terms of exposure to educationally and socially significant materials and resources. The selection mechanism, whatever it might be, undoubtedly places students based on their current level of development and the breadth and depth of the exposure they've had to the educational process that places them. In other words, the mechanism or process probably measures what they already know, or what they've been exposed to. This translates, in a real sense, to their socio-economic class, but does not measure their real academic potential. I have grave doubts, therefore, about whether attempts are made to determine their actual ability to learn a wide range of academic and intellectual materials. Their placement, wherever it happens to be, becomes a fait accompli, setting in motion a set of dynamics and circumstances destined to keep them there.

Many students who are placed in classes designated for so-called "slow learners" or "at-risk" are seen and treated as problems. Because of their personal behaviors, characteristics and styles, they are perceived as unmanageable and, therefore, controlling them is the primary objective for segregating them into less challenging and less rigorous learning tracks. These behaviors, characteristic and styles often are exaggerated by those making the placements, and much of what the teacher does for and with these students is in response to them and the perceptions they have about these students.

Many of the students are free-spirited, talkative and rambunctious; some have irrepressible energies and personalities. So, controlling them takes precedence over their academic learning. When the focus is on controlling them, often driven by fear and a lack of understanding them, a battle royal is likely to ensue, with the preponderance of instructional time spent negotiating the relationship between the teacher and the students. It will be difficult for the teacher and the students to coexist if there is not mutual respect, some basis of trust and the students feeling that the teacher is *personally invested* in their learning. Students want to know that the teacher genuinely cares about them, is concerned about them, respects them and attempts to understand them. If these enabling conditions do not exist, the students probably will become low achievers, regardless of their academic aptitude. They experience the situation as dictatorial, punitive and oppressive, and will find every way possible to be defiant, recalcitrant and uncooperative, suppressing their desire to learn, without realizing or caring that, ultimately, they are hurting themselves. This often leads to many of them being suspended or expelled. There are examples of these students being absent, with combined excused and un-excused, more than half the school term. This clearly adds nothing to their academic achievement, and further widens the achievement gap.

Some students are not placed in so-called "slow learner" or "at-risk" classes because they find it difficult to learn; they are there because they find it difficult to behave. I suspect that it is rare for schools to make distinctions between these students and, therefore, treat them all the same. This undoubtedly adds to some of the problems in these learning arrangements. With few exceptions, these students can learn almost anything they are expected to learn, are inspired to learn, and believe it is in their interest to learn. The issue is how to help them structure an environment that helps them take control of their behavior, without the teacher trying to. And the students who find it difficult to learn must be provided an environment that is conducive for their specific learning issues. When the two groups of students are placed together and treated the same, neither group is likely to make much progress in resolving their educational challenges.

This highlights the problem of how different kinds of classrooms, in many obvious and not-so-obvious ways, provide students with different kinds of learning experiences. Some enhance the learning process for students, while others interfere with it and, unwittingly, help to increase the achievement gap between groups of students. The unintentional creation of this educational inequality negates or minimizes the probability of achieving excellence and high achievement for all students.

For students who have difficulty learning, placing them in a supposedly "slow-learner" class or its equivalent, without the proper compensatory intervention, is tantamount to purposely exacerbating an existing problem, especially if the learning environment is disruptive, the instructional time is limited and the appropriate learning materials are non-existent. That students do not gain any academic and intellectual ground under these conditions should not be surprising. In fact, it should be expected that they will not, and surprising if they do. The difficulties of their plight are compounded by the fact that many of the teachers assigned to work with them do not have the necessary educational background and instructional experience to help these students in any meaningful way. Moreover, it seems that the teachers with the least amount of relevant experience and qualifications are assigned to work with the students, while logic dictates that the exact opposite would be true. This additional problem is often overlooked when assessing factors that might contribute to the achievement gap.

From my experience with several teachers working with "at-risk" students, I've determined, and I believe rather accurately, that some, if not all, would not prefer the assignment if they had a choice. In fact, many jokingly refer to the assignment as, "The Combat Zone!" I suspect that these negative feelings carryover into how they interact with the students and how they structure the learning environment for them. Many of these students already see their isolation and separation from the rest of the school in a very negative light. They see and experience the differential treatment and will tell you that it fills them with anger, affects their attitude about school, their motivation to learn, and their outlook about themselves and about life in general.

Teachers who want to work with "at-risk" students often have difficulties finding the administrative, financial, informational, parental and structural support needed for them to be more successful with the students. Students who learn at a slower rate find, in many ways, that the educational system that was created for them, in reality, has written them off as unworthy of a quality education. Notwithstanding the absence of supportive mechanisms, the teachers and students, by and large, are able to accomplish impressive feats. Just think of what they could do if the issues of the achievement gap were approached and resolved a little differently! Many of these teachers have accepted their work with these students as their calling, and they have helped the students to become outstanding academic performers and contributing members to society.

It seems that anytime there is a hierarchical exposure and learning arrangement, those at the top will be advantaged and favored, and those at the bottom will be disadvantaged and disfavored. This arrangement helps to create and perpetuate the achievement gap that it, presumably, was established to eliminate. If this is true, one has to ask: Why does the practice continue? Historically, the argument was that students learn best in homogeneous ability groupings. I know the anecdotal evidence does not support the assumption, and I feel rather confident that the empirical evidence does not support it either.

I've advocated and recommended that compensatory interventions and remediation occur in the traditional classroom, through the use of academically, educationally and socially important learning materials, and within the context of a *user-relevant* learning environment. This will provide all students access and exposure to concepts, ideas and knowledge valued by society. I believe that erroneous assumptions are made about what different kinds of students are capable of learning, and what kinds of information and knowledge are most appropriate for them. Therefore, isolating and separating students by ability groupings is an easy way of accommodating assumptions, and it presupposes that students will learn better in homogeneous groupings. To be sure, accommodating the current capabilities of all students within the same instructional framework is more difficult for the teacher because it will, or may, require additional work and detailed planning. However, if some students are denied the full range of developmental and learning opportunities and an equal exposure to educationally relevant information and knowledge, gaps in their achievement level is inevitable, as measured against those students who received the full range. Their level of achievement, in reality, will reflect their position or placement on the educational hierarchy or stratification, and that should not be surprising. Many of the students face some daunting challenges, but they are not challenges that are insurmountable.

Therefore, the wisdom of the current system has to be questioned and a new paradigm will have to be devised and implemented to ensure equal access and educational excellence for all students. The current system portrays and touts equal educational access and opportunity, which, in reality, is a façade and does not exist. When this is done, I am confident that the minority achievement gaps will be reduced and, ultimately, eliminated because the current structure and system that creates and sustains it will have been eliminated. Maintaining the current system while expecting different results is delusional!

9

WHAT PARENTS MUST DO

James Baldwin said, "Children have never been good at listening to their elders, but they've never failed to imitate them."

Spending time in and around schools can be very insightful and instructive for many reasons, not the least of which is firsthand knowledge and understanding of all the influences on the *process* of education. One of the most profound influences, positive and negative, is the role parents play in setting the expectations, tone and tenor for their children. In many instances, unfortunately, the only role many parents play is one that is destructive, negative and self-defeating for their child or children; but they blame the teachers and the educational system for the child's lack of academic and personal successes.

This point was made abundantly clear recently during an incident at a high school early one morning. I had driven for more that two hours to be there before 8 A. M. When I arrived, there were several police cruisers in front of the main office area, signaling to me that something untoward was happening. After entering the main lobby and maneuvering my way through the throng of students to sign-in with the receptionist in the inner office, I caught echoes of a heated discussion between several police officers, a young man and a woman, as they stood in the midst of several students onlookers and administrative personnel trying to convince the students to continue moving.

Shortly after pushing my way into the inner office and signing in, the warring parties, who were still engaged in verbal combat, made their way into the office also and went down a small corridor to some other inner offices. Within seconds, there was a lot of screaming and apparent scuffling taking place. The young man scrambled out into the inner office corridor, holding his face and crying, with the police in hot pursuit. The police apprehended the young man and wrestled him back into an inner office. A few minutes later, the young man was escorted out of the office, crying and in handcuffs, and was placed into one of the cruisers. Within seconds the woman was also escorted out, screaming that she had not done anything wrong, and she was placed into another cruiser.

I later learned that the young man was caught on premises using a cell phone the previous day. He knew that was a violation of school rules, so the phone was confiscated. According to several eye witnesses, the young man went into a fit of anger and kicked a door, breaking the glass in it. He was instructed not to come to school the next day unless he had a parent or guardian with him. He was also informed that the phone and an estimate for the cost of repairing would be given to that person, and that if he came to school with a cell phone again, he would be suspended. The young man had received several disciplinary actions the short time he had been at that school, and this incident was a major infraction of school rules.

Apparently, the woman, who was the young man's mother, disagreed with the school's rules and was defending her son's actions. She went so far as to try to push her way into an office where the police were questioning the young man about the door-kicking incident. When she pushed her way in, the young man attempted to get physical with the officers. He was "maced" or pepper sprayed, causing his mother to go ballistic, and resulting in both of them being arrested.

I also later learned from the principal that this was the *third* high school the young man had been in that year, and everywhere he had been, there were problems involving him that neither he nor his mother had accepted any responsibility. They had blamed all of the problems on racists principals or racism in the schools. That may have been the case. However, the young man was African-American, and the principals at all three schools he had attended were African-American also. The principal at the current school was giving him a chance to get back on track and accepted him with a clean slate. The principal's attitude was that he had bent over backwards to help the young man and to get him and is mother to take responsibility for the young man's actions, all to no avail. Now, he would let the juvenile justice system take care of the problem.

It is often hard for parents to accept that their children could do anything wrong, even when the evidence is overwhelming that they did. Children are smart enough to know that if their parents continuously come to their defense, especially when the evidence is stacked against, they are not likely to change their wayward actions and behaviors. Then it becomes a game for them to see what and how much they can do and get away with.

Notwithstanding whether the physical separation of the young man and is mother during the questioning was appropriate, if in fact that's what happened, it appears to me that there was a fundamental problem with having to find a school that would have to accede to and to accommodate the young man's inappropriate behaviors. That those behaviors played out in a way that resulted in him and his mother being arrested is quite unfortunate. More unfortunate, however, is the fact that neither he nor his mother, apparently, knew or understood, on any rational level, the behaviors required for him to be successful in his school experiences. If neither he nor his mother had learned after the three previous unsuccessful attempts, when were they going to learn?

I believe most educators enter the profession with a great deal of optimism, but give up in frustration after numerous experiences of feeling that their efforts will not make a difference with some of the students they encounter. Some students make a sport out of disrespecting some educators; and my suspicion is that many of their parents probably exhibit some of the same attitudes and behaviors when they were students. They have developed the attitude somewhere along the way that they are learning to benefit the teachers and the educational system, rather than learning to benefit themselves. This way of thinking can only lead to a very tragic outcome for the parents and the child.

Teachers are human, too! Why should they want to help a student who is a constant source of conflict and problems, and their parents, rather than trying to help resolve the conflict and problems, only add to them by their attitudes and behaviors? It doesn't matter how much knowledge and how many skills a teacher might possess if the disruptive student makes it impossible to demonstrate them.

Most parents and many educators do not understand that there is a strong correlation between students' academic failure and their aggressive, disruptive and violent behaviors. Moreover, if parents believe that their children cannot succeed in school, not valuing academic success, cognitive development and education reduces their feelings of failure. Parents' behaviors and dysfunctional values are transmitted to their children, since children tend to emulate or model their parents' behaviors and values. This symbiotic relationship and vicious cycle can create inter-generational problems that permeate large segments of entire communities, inducing them to develop fatalistic attitudes about the world generally, and about themselves specifically. The behaviors that emanate from this psychological disposition are predictable, with individuals acquiring short-term orientations, i. e., living for the moment, developing a "get-over" mentality, expressing identity through exaggerated interactions, and developing oppositional characteristics to aggravate the dominate cultural norms.

Parents must understand how their attitudes and behaviors, intentionally or unintentionally, influence their children. While it may be difficult, but not impossible, for them to change, they can and must play a major role in shaping their children's attitudes and behaviors. Parent must do several basic things early on in their children's academic, cognitive and moral development. Included are:

- Teach them a sense of personal responsibility. Children must learn from their parents that they are responsible for their successes and failures; and that they will be held accountable for their behaviors and their choices. When parents constantly bail children out of predicaments they get themselves in, the children will learn that their parents will come to their defense, even when they wrong.

- Set boundaries / limits. Children need and, in fact, look for boundaries for their attitudes and behaviors. When there are no boundaries from those responsible for their care, children often interpret it as a lack of care and love, and begin to act out in self-destructive ways. There should be boundaries / limits on unsupervised time, such as the amount and kind of television that's watched. Parents should set high expectations and assist and induce their children to achieve them.

- Parents must demand respect from their children, and show no disrespect for teachers. I've learned that when parents bad-mouth and disrespect teachers, children are inclined to also.

- Parents must invest in their children's education. One way of doing that is by getting them involved with culturally/ socially significant activities, buying educational materials, giving them educational experiences, subscribing to educational materials, such as magazines, videos, etc. I have often said that many parents spend more money on beer and cigarettes during one weekend than they spend on their children's educational exposure during a whole year. When they send their children to school in the latest fads and fashions, but do not ensure that their children have paper and pencils for school, it is a statement about their values and what they expect of and from their children.

Finally, parents must understand that the paths their children take is determined, to a large degree, by their actions and behaviors. Children will seek their own identity and rebel against many things we hold sacred and valued. That's all part of growing up. But, participating and reinforcing their self-destructive behaviors is a form of suicide for children and homicide by parents!

10

STEP-UPP

PRE-STEP-UPP TRAINING COMMENTS:

"School is boring."

Teachers don't like us. They believe we are stupid,
so I don't even try."

"Because my friends don't try, that seems cool to me."

"Because my father never praises me,
I think I can't succeed."

"They don't teach me anything I can use in life."

"They won't explain things when you ask a question.
I just go to sleep and they leave me alone."

Educators know these young people well. They see
them dropout of school all the time. Many of these
students are African-American males reflecting a
grim statistic—more than fifty-five percent of this
group will not finish high school. However, the
dropout rate is too high among all identifiable
groups, males as well as females. All together, these
kids, described as "at-risk" or "lacking focus," make
up the vast majority of students who dropout of the
educational process very early—they simply wait
until they're old enough to leave school.

Wanting to help these young people, I used knowledge I acquired during my academic experience and my experience as a management consultant and trainer to create a program titled STEP-UPP (Success Through Effective Participation—Using Positive Potential). I also drew upon my experiences as a high school teacher and as a supervisor and manager in many corporate functions where I learned, first-hand, much about human behavioral responses to interpersonal interactions and environmental stimuli. These experiences, coupled with participants' comments from organizational and personal development training sessions I conducted—I should have had this training twenty years ago—this training has changed my life—were incentives for me to positively change the lives of young adults as soon as possible.

BELIEVING SMART IS EASY

Many students believe that there is an inverse relationship between smartness and effort. In other words, they think that if you are smart, you don't have to apply effort or work hard; and if you have to apply effort or work hard, you must not be smart. They learn some of this through the social environment and group interactions. Moreover, those who share this belief are more likely to form alliances and bonds around what is known as a social comparison process (Festinger, L., 1954), and this often results in suppressing the overall achievement of the entire group. To prevent this, the STEP-UPP process aims to step in to convince these students that, in order for them to *get* smart, they have to give effort or work hard.

WHAT STEP-UPP DOES

The goal of the program is to close the achievement gap between those who do well academically and those who do not. However, trying to get students who are "at-risk" or "lacking focus" to achieve academically without addressing their emotional and social need is counterproductive because these must be strengthened first to provide the foundation for their intellectual development. Therefore, the program sets out to create an environment that *invites* the student to learn. Each session is structured to encourage and support academic and intellectual gains by supporting positive academic and social behaviors. By the end, these are the objectives STEP-UPP desires for these students:

- To better understand themselves, others and their environment

- To achieve self-respect and respect for others

- To learn to maintain a positive attitude

- To meet daily challenges and to overcome negative thoughts and behaviors

- To understand the link between effort and academic success and

- To make daily progress toward becoming successful and secure adults

Finally, it's been heartening to have students ask if they can be involved in STEP-UPP everyday, or for the remainder of the school term, after they've participated in only the first session of a nine-week program. We believe that this is because STEP-UPP is student-centered, judgment-free and achievement-oriented.

CREATING THE RIGHT ENVIRONMENT

Ideally, each session should take place in a setting where students feel *psychologically safe* to explore their beliefs, feelings and values. The facilitator is largely responsible for creating this atmosphere, as she will instill a sense of non-judgment acceptance from the beginning. Training for the facilitators and a comprehensive Facilitator's Guide show how to use the tools and how to structure the environment for the group activities to achieve this feeling of psychological safety. It should be noted here that STEP-UPP does not, however, permit students to use the session to gripe, blame and find excuses for not taking personal responsibility for their lives, or try to gain social status and / or group leadership positions.

THE DESIGN OF THE PROGRAM

STEP-UPP lasts nine weeks, with one two-hour session each week. The target population is "at-risk" junior high school students needing special help with emotional and social learning to improve the academic performance. However, it can be extended for a longer period of time, and it has been modified to meet the needs of elementary and high school boys and girls. The process uses activities such as group discussions, relevant audio and video cassettes, assignments from the training manual each participant receives, weekly goal setting and self-monitoring, and skill-building strategies. While there is no specific emphasis on learning skills and intellectual development, there is a module on "The Elements of Academic Success" to complement the strong link between emotional growth and academic achievement.

HOW STEP-UPP OPERATES

At the first session, students are encouraged to learn and *internalize* the STEP-UPP CREED:

I believe my life has value, that my existence has purpose, and that I have the ability to change.
I believe that all humanity is my kin, and that to mistreat anyone is to mistreat myself.

I believe that it is my responsibility to rid myself of self-limiting thoughts and self-defeating and self-destructive behaviors. It is through a positive mental attitude and a belief in my self-worth that I can grow in confidence and learn self-respect.

I believe that I must take advantage of every opportunity to learn and to prepare myself for the future. If I am the best, I can go as far as my skills and capabilities will take me; and it will be difficult for anyone to deny me the opportunity to show what I can do.

I cannot become consumed by material possessions because they do not define me. My accomplishments, attitudes, contributions and knowledge are the true measure of who I really am.

I believe I can be a positive influence on my family and friends and a role model to those who look up to me. Making others proud of me and helping others are goals worthy of my pursuit.

I pledge to STEP-UPP to the challenges before me, for it is through my attitude, behaviors and effort that I can excel and achieve success and personal mastery.

(C) 1995 Wilbur L. Brower

Most of the students learn the creed within a week, probably because it presents them with so many positive options, which is a distinct change for many of them.

At every session the students are encouraged to set one academic and one behavioral / social goal each week, and then to self-monitor how well they progress toward those goals. The training manual contains goal-setting forms and forms for the students to record their insights and observations about their goals. Because they are encouraged to set reachable goals, the students begin to understand that achieving success is an incremental process that requires effort. Their small successes build their confidence and motivate them to try harder.

Over the course of the nine weeks, teachers complete an assessment form for each student regarding his or her progress in academics, behaviors, discipline, effort, homework, participation and respect. These ratings are from one (1) (Unsatisfactory) to four (4) (Excellent). Meanwhile, during the sessions, the facilitator reminds the students often that teachers are their advocates and allies, not their adversaries and enemies. One result is that students are encouraged to thank their teachers for teaching them. Not surprisingly, students who do this report a change in their teachers' attitude toward them, causing these students to change their attitudes toward their teachers. This mutually reinforcing process keeps teachers and the students engaged in the students' development. The students tend to try harder, and the teachers take a more personal interest in the students' personal successes. At the same time, the goal-setting process helps students to learn that achieving is an attitude and a behavior, and that it also involves self-discipline.

Videos, such as *Cadillac Dreams* and one made by *East Jersey Lifer's Group* about life in prison, are used to help students examine self-defeating attitudes and behaviors that often have severe legal and social consequences. They also have in-dept discussions of questions such as:

1. What do you think it would take for you to improve your school behavior?

2. If you worked really hard, how well do you think you could do in school?

3. What do you think it means to be a man or a woman?

4. If you had one very important thing you wanted to accomplish in the next six months, how would you do it?

These training aids and techniques, along with many others, are used to help students internalize the Formula for Success (**Working Smart** plus **Having Determination** minus **Self-Defeating Behaviors** equals **Personal Mastery**).

POST STEP-UPP TRAINING COMMENTS:

"Talking with you really woke me up to thinking about my life and how I live it. Thank you for spending your time—because of you, I care."

"As a result of the program, I will take advantage of every opportunity that will prepare me for the future."

"You've helped me a lot since you've been here at school. I don't sell drugs anymore because you taught me to set goals for myself. Thanks for everything."

"It was really cool that you've come and changed my actions toward other people. I'm doing well in school and passing classes. The way you explained your life story changed mine and my peers' lives."

"I like when you played that music. It made me understand that music is just music."

SOURCES AND
SUGGESTED READING

Canfield, J. (September, 1990). "Improving Students' Self-Esteem." *Educational Leadership* 48:1., 48-50.

Ceci, S. (1990). *On Intelligence...More or Less: A Bio-Ecological Treatise on Intellectual Development.* Englewood, NJ: Prentice-Hall

Comer, J.,& Poussaint, A. (1992). *Raising Black Children – Two Leading Psychiatrists Confront the Educational, Social and Emotional Problems Facing Black Children.* New York: Plume Books.

Damon, W. (1991). *Great Expectations – Overcoming the Culture of Indulgence in America's Homes and Schools.* New York: The Free Press.

Diener, C, & Dweck,C. (1978). "An Analysis of Learned Helplessness: Continuous Changes in Performance, Strategy, and Achievement Cognitions Following Failure." *Journal of Personality and Social Psychology.* 36: 351-362.

Duncan, G. & Brook-Gunn, J. (Eds). (1997). *The Consequences of Growing Up Poor.* New York: Russell Sage Foundation.

Festinger, L. (1954). "A Theory of Social Comparison Processes." Human Relations 7: 117-140

Gurian, M. (1999). *The Good Son – Shaping the Moral Development of Our Boys and Young Men.* New York: Jeremy P. Tarcher / Putman.

Hunter, M. (1967). *Teacher More, Faster – A Programmed Book.* Thousand Oaks, CA

Karr-Morse, R. & Wiley, M. (1997). *Ghosts for the Nursery – Tracing the Roots of Violence.* New York: The Atlantic Monthly Press.

Kotula, R. (1997). *Inside the Brain – Revolutionary Discoveries of How the Brain Works.* Kansas City, KS: Andrews Mc Meel Publishing

Neito, S. (1992). *Affirming Diversity – The Socio-Political Context of Multi-cultural Education.* White Plains, NY: Longman Publishers.

Ogbu, J. (1985). "A Cultural Ecology of Competence Among Inner-City Blacks" in M. B. Spencer, G. K. Brookins, & W. R. Allen (Eds.). *Beginnings: The Social and Affective Development of the Black Child.* Hillsdale, NJ: Erlbaum

Pollack, W. (1998). *Real Boys – Rescuing Our Sons from the Myths of Boyhood.* New York, NY: Random House.

Reglin, G, (1990). "A Model Program for Educating At-Risk Students." *Technological Horizons in Education Journal,* 17, (6), 65-67.

Sharron, H. (1987). *Changing Children's Mind – Feuerstein's Revolution in the Teaching of Intelligence.* London: Souvenir Press (E&A), Ldt.

Stevenson, H. & Stigler, J. (1992). *The Learning Gap – Why Our Schools Are Failing and What We Can Learn from the Japanese and Chinese Education.* New York, NY: Summit Books.

ABOUT THE AUTHOR

Dr. Wil Brower is an educational and management consultant and trainer, specializing in human and organizational development. He is also an educator, professional facilitator, lecturer, mediator and writer. Some of his writings on the subjects of organizational and personal effectiveness have appeared in *Harvard Business Review* (Nov.-Dec., 1996) and *Cultural Diversity at Work* (January, 1997). One of his major presentations was published in *Vital Speeches of the Day* (Feb 15, 2000). He is the author of *A Little Book of Big Principles--Values and Virtues for a More Successful Life* (1998); *Traffic Signs on the Road of Life (2012;* and co-author of *Personal Care Journal: The Adult Years – A Ready-Reference of Vital Information* (2001).

Through W. Brower & Associates, Dr. Brower has provided consulting and training services for organizations such as Hewlett-Packard Corporation, Marriott Corporation, The University of Memphis, DuPont Pharmaceuticals, Dow Chemical Company, U. S. Veterans Administration, the State of Arkansas, Raleigh News and Observer, U.S. Army Corps of Engineers and the U. S. Postal Service.

Through his non-profit organization, Institute for Youth Development and Educational Resources, (IYDER), Inc., Dr. Brower develops and facilitates training modules for students at-risk of academic and personal failure and for adults who work with these students. His organizations are based in Trenton, NC.

www.ingramcontent.com/pod-product-compliance
Lightning Source LLC
Chambersburg PA
CBHW050538280326
41933CB00011B/1637